Just for Kids

Knock Knock Jokes

Just for Kids

Knock Knock Jokes

Jessica Jacobs

www.littlemoonmedia.com

For my two precious boys who love
to laugh. You are my dream come
true. Ollie and Joshie, this is for you.

Mummy xxx

For free bonus jokes, visit:

www.littlemoonmedia.com/kk-bonus/

Contents

Let's Start Laughing!

Just for Kids

Knock knock

Who's there?

Snow

Snow who?

Snow use, I can't remember my name!

Knock knock

Who's there?

A tish

A tish who?

Bless you!

Knock knock

Who's there?

Waa

Waa who?

You sound very excited!

Knock knock

Who's there?

Yah

Yah who?

Seriously, why are you so excited?

Knock knock

Who's there?

Wooden shoe

Wooden shoe who?

Wooden shoe like to let me in?

Knock knock

Who's there?

Peek-a

Peek-a who?

No, it's not peek-a-who,

it's Peek-a-BOO!

Knock knock

Who's there?

Witches

Witches who?

Witches the way home?? I'm lost!

Knock knock

Who's there?

Juicy

Juicy who?

Juicy me standing here waiting?

Knock knock

Who's there?

None

None who?

None of your business!

Knock knock

Who's there?

Sing

Sing who?

sing the word "Who"

Knock knock

Who's there?

Icy

Icy who?

Icy what you're doing!

Knock knock

Who's there?

Stopwatch

Stopwatch who?

Stopwatch you're doing and give me a hug!

Knock knock

Who's there?

Panther

Panther who?

Panther what you wear on your legth!

Knock knock

Who's there?

Repeat

Repeat who?

Who who who who

Knock knock

Who's there?

Who who

Who who who?

Don't get so excited, it's just a joke!

Knock knock

Who's there?

Lego

Lego who?

Lego of me and I'll tell you!

Knock knock

Who's there?

Wire

Wire who?

Wire you asking me?

Knock knock

Who's there?

Any

Any who?

Anybody you'd like to let in the door!

Knock knock

Who's there?

Radio

Radio who?

Rad-io-not, here I come

Knock knock

Who's there?

Kenya

Kenya who?

Kenya open the door please?

Knock knock

Who's there?

Juno

Juno who?

Juno who I am, don't you?

Knock knock

Who's there?

Cargo

Cargo who?

Cargo beep beep, broom

broooom!!

Knock knock

Who's there?

Canoe

Canoe who?

Canoe open the door please?

Knock knock

Who's there?

I am

I am who?

Don't you know who you are?

Knock knock

Who's there?

Needle

Needle who?

Needle little help opening the door!

Knock knock

Who's there?

Ima

Ima who?

Ima getting old here, open the door!

Knock knock

Who's there?

Iva

Iva who?

Iva sore hand from knocking so much!

Knock knock

Who's there?

Police

Police who?

Police (please) let me in!

Knock knock

Who's there?

Avenue

Avenue who?

Avenue heard this one before?

Knock knock

Who's there?

Nanna

Nanna who?

Nanna your business

Knock knock

Who's there?

Boo

Boo who?

Don't cry, it's just a joke!

Will you remember me in a year?

Yes

Will you remember me in a month?

Yes

Will you remember me in a week?

Yes

Will you remember me in a day?

Yes

Will you remember me in a minute?

(person says "Yes")

Knock knock

Who's there?

Did you forget me already?

Knock knock

Who's there?

CD

CD who?

CD the person on your doorstep?

That's me!

Knock knock

Who's there?

Double

Double who?

W

Knock knock

Who's there?

Jamaican

Jamaican who?

Jamaican me crazy with all these jokes!

Knock knock

Who's there?

Seeya

Seeya who?

Seeya later alligator!

Knock knock

Who's there?

Dozen

Dozen who?

Dozen anybody want to let me in?

Knock knock

Who's there?

Spell

Spell who?

W-H-O

Knock knock

Who's there?

Interrupting Pirate

(While they ask "Interrupting Pirate who?),

say "Arrrrrrrrrr" in a loud voice

Knock knock

Who's there?

Adore

Adore who?

Adore is between us, open up!

Knock knock

Who's there?

Leaf

Leaf who?

Leaf me alone!

Knock knock

Who's there?

Somebody too short to reach the doorbell!

Knock knock

Who's there?

Bean

Bean who?

Bean away a while, but I'm back again now!

Just for Kids

Knock Knock Names

Just for Kids

Knock knock

Who's there?

Mikey

Mikey who?

Mikey doesn't fit in the lock

Knock knock

Who's there?

Howard

Howard who?

Howard I know?

Knock knock

Who's there?

Isabel

Isabel who?

Isabel necessary on a door

Knock knock

Who's there?

Luke

Luke who?

Luke though the keyhole and

you'll be able to see

Knock knock

Who's there?

Oscar

Oscar who?

Oscar silly question, get a silly answer!

Knock knock

Who's there?

Avery

Avery who?

Avery nice person. May I come in please?

Knock knock

Who's there?

Abbie

Abbie who?

Abbie stung me on my nose!

Knock knock

Who's there?

Ben

Ben who?

Ben knocking for 10 minutes, couldn't you hear me?

Knock knock

Who's there?

Noah

Noah who?

Noah good game we can play?

Knock knock

Who's there?

Harry

Harry who?

Harry up, it's freezing out here!!

Knock knock

Who's there?

Mary-lee

Mary-lee who?

Mary-lee Mary-lee Mary-lee life is but a dream

Knock knock

Who's there?

Fanny

Fanny who?

If Fanny body asks tell them I'm busy!

Knock knock

Who's there?

Noah

Noah who?

Noah way to get the door open?

Knock knock

Who's there?

Anita

Anita who?

Anita go to the toilet!! Let me in!

Knock knock

Who's there?

Frank

Frank who?

Frank you for letting me in!

Knock knock

Who's there?

Justin

Justin who?

Justin time for lunch, I'm hungry!

Knock knock

Who's there?

Wendy

Wendy who?

Wendy bell works I won't have to keep knocking!

Knock knock

Who's there?

Wanda

Wanda who?

I Wanda if you're going to let me in!

Knock knock

Who's there?

Amos

Amos who?

Amos-quito bit me - ouch!

Knock knock

Who's there?

Doris

Doris who?

Doris locked, open it up!

Knock knock

Who's there?

Will

Will who?

Will you please let me in?

It's cold out here!!

Knock knock

Who's there?

Annie

Annie who?

Annie body home?

Knock knock

Who's there?

Annie

Annie who?

Annie one you like!

Knock knock

Who's there?

Annie

Annie who?

Annie chance you want more jokes?

Knock knock

Who's there?

Philip

Philip who?

Philip my bag with Halloween

candy please!

Knock knock

Who's there?

Lena

Lena who?

Lena bit closer so you can see me!

Knock knock

Who's there?

Watson

Watson who?

Watson TV tonight?

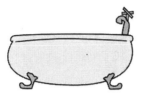

Knock knock

Who's there?

Dwayne

Dwayne who?

Dwayne the bathtub, it's going to overflow!!

Knock knock

Who's there?

Ken

Ken who?

Ken I come in please?

Knock knock

Who's there?

Sadie

Sadie who?

Sadie magic word and I will disappear!

Knock Knock Food

Just for Kids

Knock knock

Who's there?

Ice Cream

Ice Cream who?

Ice Cream if you won't let me come in!

Knock knock

Who's there?

Sultan

Sultan who?

Sultan pepper!

Knock knock

Who's there?

Icing

Icing who?

Icing you a lovely song

(then sing your favorite song!)

Knock knock

Who's there?

Ketchup

Ketchup who?

Ketchup with me and I'll tell you

(quickly run away!)

Knock knock

Who's there?

Olive

Olive who?

Olive you so much!!

Knock knock

Who's there?

Lettuce

Lettuce who?

Lettuce in please, it's raining out here!

Knock knock

Who's there?

Broccoli

Broccoli who?

You're funny, broccoli don't have

a last name!

Knock knock

Who's there?

Honeydew

Honeydew who?

Honeydew you love me?

Knock knock

Who's there?

Figs

Figs who?

Figs the doorbell, it's broken!

Knock knock

Who's there?

Apple

Apple who?

Knock knock

Who's there?

Apple

Apple who?

Knock knock

Who's there?

Apple

Apple who?

Knock knock

Who's there?

Orange

Orange who?

Orange you glad I got rid of that annoying apple?

Knock knock

Who's there?

Water

Water who?

Water funny way to answer the door!

Knock knock

Who's there?

Butter

Butter who?

Butter open the door to find out!

Knock knock

Who's there?

Ice-cream soda

Ice-cream soda who?

Ice-cream soda whole world will hear me!

Knock knock

Who's there?

Donut

Donut who?

Donut ask, it's a secret…ssshhhhh!

Knock knock

Who's there?

Hummus

Hummus who?

Humm-us a song will you please?

Knock knock

Who's there?

Gorilla

Gorilla who?

Gorilla me a hamburger, I'm starving!

Knock knock

Who's there?

Orange

Orange who?

Orange you sick of all these knock knock jokes?

Knock knock

Who's there?

Water

Water who?

Water you doing in my house?

Knock knock

Who's there?

Cash

Cash who?

No thank you I'd rather have a peanut

Knock knock

Who's there?

Berry

Berry who?

Berry nice to meet you! Can I come in now?

Just for Kids

Knock Knock

Animals

Just for Kids

Knock knock

Who's there?

Cows

Cows who?

Don't be silly, cows Moo!

Knock knock

Who's there?

Kanga

Kanga who?

Actually it's kangaROO!

Knock knock

Who's there?

Interrupting cow

(as the person says "Interrupting cow who?",

say **"Mooooooo"** in a loud voice!)

Knock knock

Who's there?

Who

Who who?

Are you pretending to be an owl?

Knock knock

Who's there?

Cows go

Cows go who?

No silly, cows go moo

Knock knock

Who's there?

Goat

Goat who?

Goat to the door and you'll see

Knock knock

Who's there?

Some bunny

Some bunny who?

Some bunny ate all my carrots!

Knock knock

Who's there?

A T-rex

A T-rex who?

What??

There's a T-rex at your door and you want to know his name??

Knock knock

Who's there?

Lion

Lion who?

Stop lion around and let me in!

Knock Knock

Holidays

Just for Kids

Knock knock

Who's there?

Mary

Mary who?

Mary Christmas!

Just for Kids

Knock knock

Who's there?

Ho Ho

Ho Ho who?

No, Santa says Ho Ho HO!

Just for Kids

Thank You!

Thank you so much for purchasing this book. I hope you have had as much fun reading it as I have had creating it!

I would be very grateful if you could help me out by **leaving a quick review** on Amazon. Reviews really help people to find my book.

Also, as a **free bonus** to this book, for a limited time I'd like to send you a gift of some extra jokes. Just go to:

www.littlemoonmedia.com/kk-bonus/

Keep on laughing,

Jessica x

49232148R00055

Made in the USA
San Bernardino, CA
17 May 2017